LEGENDS OF WARFARE

NAVAL

Liberty Ships

America's Merchant Marine Transport in World War II

DAVID DOYLE

SCHIFFER MILITARY

4880 Lower Valley Road   Atglen, PA 19310

Designed by Justin Watkinson
Technical Layout by Jack Chappell
Type set in Impact/Minion Pro/Univers LT Std

ISBN: 978-0-7643-5959-0
Printed in China

Published by Schiffer Publishing, Ltd.
4880 Lower Valley Road
Atglen, PA 19310
Phone: (610) 593-1777; Fax: (610) 593-2002
E-mail: Info@schifferbooks.com
www.schifferbooks.com

For our complete selection of fine books on this and related subjects, please visit our website at www.schifferbooks.com. You may also write for a free catalog.

Schiffer Publishing's titles are available at special discounts for bulk purchases for sales promotions or premiums. Special editions, including personalized covers, corporate imprints, and excerpts, can be created in large quantities for special needs. For more information, contact the publisher.

We are always looking for people to write books on new and related subjects. If you have an idea for a book, please contact us at proposals@schifferbooks.com.

Acknowledgments

This book would not have been possible without the generous assistance of handful of people. I am especially indebted to Tom Kailbourn, Scott Taylor, Tracy White, James Noblin, Rick Davis, Chris Hughes, and Richard Thresh. My darling wife, Denise, as always, scanned photos and served as my constant cheerleader during the frustrating times of this project.

All photos not otherwise noted are by the author.

Contents

Introduction

Just as Hitler's army marched across Europe in an effort to completely dominate the continent, his U-boats and surface raiders prowled the Atlantic in the early days of World War II. The objective of these submarines, often operating in "wolf packs," was to destroy the ships bringing critically needed supplies to England and allies in Europe. The U-boats, under *Admiral* Karl Dönitz, were incredibly successful, sinking merchant ships, with their cargoes and crews, at an alarming rate. The worst month for England was May 1941, when 125 merchant ships were lost.

British shipyards, straining to maintain and build warships, could hardly keep up with the losses. As early as September 1940, the British had sought American help with the production of cargo vessels. British envoys presented the blueprints for the *Dorington Court* to Admiral Emory Scott Land, the chairman of the United States Maritime Commission, asking that the US build duplicates of this ship en masse.

The US had prior experience mass-producing merchant ships. During World War I, the United States Shipping Board, predecessor to the US Maritime Commission, had ordered hundreds of merchant ships of a variety of designs to meet a similar need. Some were less than successful, such as hundreds of wooden ships, while others, such as the famous turbine-powered steel Hog Islanders, were widely regarded as successful.

Admiral Land felt that the British design was obsolete, relying on triple-expansion reciprocating steam engines and utilizing coal-fired boilers. Nevertheless, he consented to having slightly improved versions built in the US. On December 19, 1940, Todd Shipyards was contracted to build sixty of the improved vessels, which were referred to as Ocean-class ships. Half of these would be built in South Portland, Maine, the other half in Richmond, California.

The immediate ancestors of the Liberty ships were the sixty Ocean-class freighters built by Todd Shipyards to a slightly modified British design. *Library of Congress*

The Ocean-class ships also led the way in terms of mass-producing cargo ships during World War II. Here, five of the vessels are launched simultaneously at the Todd shipyard in Portland, Maine, on August 16, 1942. *Library of Congress*

CHAPTER 1
The Wartime Crisis

The Liberty ships were by intent not the most state-of-the-art vessels built. Rather, the ships were designed to be built rapidly, to utilize technology that not only was proven but could be understood, built, operated, and maintained by men who may have had years of hands-on experience but little formal education, and venerable facilities.

While the World War I–era Hog Islanders had turbine power plants, the Liberty ships seemingly took a step backward with their triple-expansion reciprocating engines. In reality, the massive 170-ton engine, which turned at a modest 76 rpm, was much less expensive to manufacture than the steam turbine and associated reduction gear sets were. Further, such engines had seen widespread use not only at sea, but with industrial use ashore, and thus were familiar to many. Also, while the nation's entire output of naval turbines had been allocated for warships, no fewer than eighteen firms produced the 21-foot-long, 19-foot-tall reciprocating engine of the Liberty ships.

Not only the engine but the entire vessel was designed for rapid construction. Welded rather than the laborious riveted construction practice was used. Further, the design was such that large sections could be prefabricated and subsequently rapidly assembled.

The keel for the first Liberty ship was laid on April 30, 1941, at Bethlehem-Fairfield Shipyards Inc. in Baltimore, Maryland. Five months later, that vessel, the SS *Patrick Henry*, and thirteen other merchant ships were launched on September 27, 1941, which was dubbed "Liberty Fleet Day." President Franklin Roosevelt launched the *Patrick Henry*.

While in time some of the Liberty ships would be taken over by the US Navy (and even the Army), when built the ships bore the appellation "SS"—indicating Steam Ship—rather than "USS," or United States Ship. United States Ships are operated by the Navy, while the Liberty ships were operated by the Merchant Marine.

The basic Liberty ship had the formal design designation of EC2-S-C1. This nomenclature indicated the following: "EC" for emergency cargo, "2" for a ship between 400 and 450 feet long, "S" for steam engines, and "C1" for design C1. While the EC2-S-C1 is the focus of this book, it should also be mentioned that the Maritime Commission also approved the construction of sixty-two Liberty tankers of type Z-ET1-S-C3, as well as twenty-four Liberty-type colliers, the EC2-S-AW1, and thirty-six were converted to ZEC-S-C5 configuration to transport boxed aircraft.

The crews of the Liberty ships were made up of Merchant Mariners; typically, thirty-eight to sixty of the skilled mariners were aboard each ship, as well as twenty to forty-one US Navy Armed Guards. The latter were aboard to man the guns. While the Navy Armed Guards were US servicemen and received such recognition and benefits, sadly it would be 1988 before the members of the Merchant Marine were similarly recognized, even though the casualty rate for the Merchant Marine was higher than those of the US armed forces.

The following series of photographs documents the construction of a Liberty ship at the Bethlehem-Fairfield Shipyards, near Baltimore, Maryland, in early 1943. Here, in a view of the building ways, the laying of the keel plates is underway. The keel plates provided the bottom structure of the backbone of the ship, to which the vertical keel soon would be attached. Lateral wooden beams support the keel plates, and scaffolding is erected to the sides. *Library of Congress*

On day three of construction of the Liberty ship, the bottom has been completed except for the forward and aft ends, as seen from above the eventual location of the bow. In the foreground, workmen are riveting the shell, the outer skin of the hull; the vertical keel runs along the center of this area. Just aft of the riveters, the inner bottom tanks, which will contain fuel or ballast, have been installed on the bottom of the hull. To the rear of the tanks, the midships lateral bulkhead is under construction. *Library of Congress*

A crane lowers the chain-locker assembly, weighing 16 tons, into position at the forepeak while workmen help nudge it into place. The chain locker would hold the anchor chain. Because the success of the Allied war effort depended on placing new ships into service at a greater rate than the enemy could sink ships, the emphasis was on achieving the fastest possible time between the laying of the keel and the launching of the ship. Therefore, whenever possible, prefabricated assemblies and structures such as this chain locker were used, saving precious assembly time on the building ways. *Library of Congress*

The bow of a Liberty ship takes shape on the No. 3 Way at Bethlehem-Fairfield Shipyards. To the sides of the bow is wooden scaffolding, and below the bow are the beams and shoring that support the ship. A motivational poster reminds the shipyard workers of the important part they are playing in the defense of their country. To the left is one of the cranes that hoisted heavy materials and placed them where needed in the hull. *Library of Congress*

On the fourteenth day of the construction of a Liberty ship, the upper deck has been constructed and mast houses and the after deckhouse are in place. Installation of electrical conduits and engine and boiler room piping is underway. In the foreground on the forecastle is the windlass, the mechanism that raises and lowers the anchor and operates the hawsers, the cables with which the ship is hauled in to a dock. *Library of Congress*

Two days before the launching of this Liberty ship at Bethlehem-Fairfield's shipyard, all structural work is nearing completion. A platform and splinter shield for it have been erected on the forecastle. Underwater installations are finished, and the hull has been painted. *Library of Congress*

After just twenty-four days of construction, the day has come for the launching of the Liberty ship in April 1943. The christening platform has been placed around the lower part of the bow. Red, white, and blue bunting has been placed on the top of the bow along with a temporary placard of an eagle, with the words "Ships for Victory." *Library of Congress*

The stern and propeller of the Liberty ship SS *F. A. C. Muhlenberg* are shown shortly before its launching at Bethlehem-Fairfield Shipyards. The rudder and the propeller are immobilized with locks to prevent damage as the ship enters the water. The *Muhlenberg* was laid down on February 24, 1942, and was launched on May 13 of that year. The Maritime Commission assigned a hull number to each Liberty ship: the *F. A. C. Muhlenberg*'s was number 81. *Library of Congress*

When SS *Patrick Henry* was launched, as seen here in a photograph dated September 27, 1941, that ship had set a new Liberty ship construction record of less than five months from keel laying to launching; previous Liberty ships had taken upward of seven months from keel laying to launching. By early 1943, that time had been cut down to, in many cases, about two weeks. *Library of Congress*

SS *Richard Henry Lee* (*left*), Maritime Commission hull number 18, was laid down July 15, 1941, at Bethlehem-Fairfield and launched December 6, 1941, while her neighbor, SS *John Randolph*, hull number 19, was laid down July 15, 1941, and launched December 30, 1941. They are shown at a fitting-out dock at Baltimore, where the upper structures not present at the time of launching were constructed. *Library of Congress*

SS *Charles Carroll*, Maritime Commission hull number 15, and an unidentified Liberty ship are being fitted out after launching. The dates of the *Charles Carroll*'s laying down and launching are not recorded, but the ship was built at Bethlehem-Fairfield and was delivered on January 19, 1942. *Library of Congress*

Two Liberty ships, including SS *Roger B. Taney* in the background, are undergoing completion at a fitting-out dock at Bethlehem-Fairfield. The numbers on both sides of the *Taney*'s bow and the nearer ship's stern are draft marks, indicating the distance to the bottom of the keel. *Library of Congress*

The Liberty ship SS *David Davis* was launched on November 6, 1942, at Permanente Metals Corporation's Yard No. 1, Richmond, California. Days later, on November 20, the US Navy (USN) took possession of the ship, renaming it USS *Carina* (AK-74; AK being the USN symbol for cargo ship). The ship was assigned to the Crater class of cargo ships, based on EC2-S-CI-type Liberty ships. Ultimately there were sixty-two Crater-class ships, and they were manned by USN crews and were used for delivering cargo close to combat zones. This photo shows the ship docked at San Francisco two days after the USN takeover of it, with a newly added antiaircraft gun platform along the main deck circled. In the background is the San Francisco–Oakland Bay Bridge. *National Archives via James Noblin*

A port midships photo of USS *Carina* (AK-74) at San Francisco on November 22, 1944, shows other changes in progress. Circled to the right is another new antiaircraft gun platform on a pedestal. The platform is at a height of two levels above the deck. Another new structure, a tub abreast of the smokestack, also is circled. *National Archives via James Noblin*

The aft port section of USS *Carina* is shown in another photograph from November 22, 1944. Abreast of the mizzenmast are angled racks for life rafts. At the base of the above-decks part of the mizzenmast is the mizzenmast locker, with two large cowl ventilators on top of it. To the front and the rear of the locker are steam-powered cargo winches. Above the stern of the ship is the aft deckhouse. Much of the rudder is out of the water at this point in the ship's construction. *National Archives via James Noblin*

A view from above the starboard amidships area of USS *Cassiopeia* (AK-75), originally SS *Melville W. Fuller*, includes the mainmast to the left and the foremast in the background. The masts of a Liberty ship served to support booms for loading and unloading cargo. Cowl ventilators on the mast lockers were movable to take advantage of the direction of the wind. Between the masts is the number 2 cargo hatch; the number 1 cargo hatch is to the front of the foremast. Life rafts and oars are on the rack to the right. *National Archives via James Noblin*

The amidships superstructure of USS *Cassiopeia*, also called the midships house or simply the house, is viewed from the port side in a photograph dated November 28, 1942. The structure with the windscreen over it, located to the front of the smokestack, is the auxiliary bridge, nicknamed the monkey island. In the left foreground is a tub for an antiaircraft gun, yet to be installed. On the railing to the right of the photo is a nameplate with the ship's original name, *Melville W. Fuller. National Archives via James Noblin*

The *Redfield Proctor* nameplate was still on the rail on top of the superstructure when this photo was taken on December 21, 1942. The view is from the forward port corner of the deck designated the top of the house, next to the antiaircraft gun tub on the port side. To the front of the smokestack is the frame for the cover over the auxiliary bridge, next to which is the flag bag, a metal locker with a canvas cover in which were stored the signal flags. The box-shaped structure at the center behind the life preserver is the radio antenna trunk, through which a lead from the radio antennas was channeled to the radio room below. *National Archives via James Noblin*

Another Liberty ship that was transferred to the US Navy was SS *Redfield Proctor*, which was delivered to the Navy on December 19, 1942, and renamed USS *Celeno* (AK-76). The ship is shown dockside in San Francisco on December 21, 1942, with the focus being on the forward port life-raft rack. On the rack is an eighteen-man wooden life raft, which had the appearance of a large crate. On the sides of the raft were rope loops for men in the water to hang on to. *National Archives via James Noblin*

The *Celeno*, formerly the *Redfield Proctor*, is viewed from the forward starboard corner of the top of the house on December 21, 1942. To the right are the smokestack and two cowl ventilators; in the center background is a gun tub and the starboard nameplate for the *Redfield Proctor*. Below the level of the top of the house is the bridge deck, and then the next level down is the boat deck, with two lifeboats and their davits visible to the lower left. *National Archives via James Noblin*

Compare this view from the forward starboard corner of the top of the house of USS *Cassiopeia* (formerly *Melville W. Fuller*) with the preceding photo, taken from a similar perspective on USS *Celeno*. In most respects the features are the same, except the *Cassiopeia* lacked a gun tub near the rear of the top of the house. In the distance is the aft deckhouse. *National Archives via James Noblin*

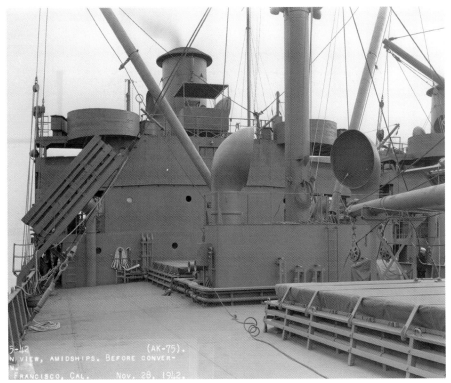

The superstructure of USS *Cassiopeia* (AK-75) is seen from the starboard side of the main deck. To the left on the inclined rack is a life raft, stenciled on the side with "No. 1" and "18 PERSONS." The auxiliary bridge is on the top of the house. In the foreground is the number 2 cargo hatch, with the number 3 cargo hatch visible between the mainmast and the front of the superstructure. *National Archives via James Noblin*

Facing toward the stern of USS *Celeno* (AK-76) from the aft port corner of the top of the house, the gable-roofed structure directly below, on the boat deck, is above the engine room and includes skylights in the form of hinged doors. Two large cowl ventilators are on the structure. Two more such ventilators are toward the rear of the boat deck. *National Archives via James Noblin*

This photo was taken on USS *Cassiopeia* to the front of the aft deckhouse, looking toward the rear of the superstructure on November 28, 1942. In the right foreground is the number 5 cargo hatch, the rearmost of the cargo hatches. To the front of that hatch are two winches and the lower part of the mizzenmast. Farther forward is the number 4 cargo hatch. *National Archives via James Noblin*

USS *Cassiopeia* (AK-75) is viewed off the starboard quarter while at anchor off San Francisco on December 19, 1942. On the platform over the aft deckhouse is a 5-inch/38-caliber dual-purpose gun, effective both against aerial and surface targets. To the immediate front of that gun mount are two 20 mm antiaircraft guns in gun tubs. *National Archives via James Noblin*

USS *Cassiopeia* is seen from the port side off San Francisco on December 19, 1942. A 3-inch antiaircraft gun was mounted on the platform over the forecastle. Loaded and secured on the main deck were several landing craft of various types. Two days after this photo was taken, *Cassiopeia* would depart for Nouméa, New Caledonia, with supplies for pursuing military operations in the Solomon Islands. *National Archives via James Noblin*

In a third view of *Cassiopeia* on December 19, 1942, two of the booms of the foremast are deployed, while the other two booms of that mast are stowed in the upright position. The mainmast of this ship was not equipped with booms at this time, while all of the mizzenmast's booms are in the stowed position. On each corner of the top of the house is a 20 mm antiaircraft gun, fully elevated, with a cover over it. *National Archives via James Noblin*

Conversion of USS *Carina* (AK-74) for use as a USN cargo ship has been completed at San Francisco in this photo dated December 12, 1942. Soon the ship would leave San Francisco bound for the Solomon Islands. The 5-inch/38-caliber gun mount over the stern gave the ship a potent defensive weapon against attacking aircraft and surface ships. *National Archives via James Noblin*

The *Carina* is observed off its port bow in early December 1942. New features added during the ship's conversion to US Navy use are circled, including addition antiaircraft gun platforms, new lights and spotlights on the masts, and other details. *National Archives via James Noblin*

Carina is viewed from its port side in San Francisco on December 2, 1942, following its conversion, with recent USN additions circled. For example, in the aft corner of the boat deck, a stack of two life rafts has been positioned. Slightly forward of the life rafts, the new gun tub on the top of the house and the pedestal that supports it, extending down to the boat deck, are circled. *National Archives via James Noblin*

The port side of *Carina* is viewed from the superstructure to the bow in another photograph dated December 2, 1942. Even a recent addition as minor as small hose holders on the sides of the foremast locker and the mainmast locker has been indicated by circles. *National Archives via James Noblin*

The aft part of *Carina* is seen from the port side. Circled additions include a hose holder on the side of the mizzenmast locker, a boom stowed on the side of the hull, a motor launch stored on the deck, and new gun mounts atop the aft deckhouse. At the top of the mizzenmast, a crow's nest with a side door and a roof has been installed. A crow's nest on the top of the foremast already was a standard feature of Liberty ships. Above the crow's nest on the mizzenmast, a small yardarm near the top of the mizzen topmast is circled. *National Archives via James Noblin*

USS *Cassiopeia* (AK-75) is viewed from the port side at San Francisco on December 10, 1942, after its conversion to US Navy specifications. The photo apparently was taken from the roof of a building along a dock, so features below the main deck are not in view. Almost twenty revisions are circled. One of the more interesting ones is the addition of extensive ventilation louvers to the gable-roofed structure containing the skylights. *National Archives via James Noblin*

The port side of the superstructure of the *Cassiopeia* is seen from the same apparent rooftop, from a more forward perspective. Monkey island, the auxiliary bridge, is visible between the two forward gun tubs on the top of the house. A newly installed crow's nest is on top of the mizzenmast, although partially hidden by a boom. To the left, at the front of the superstructure, a hatch cover with a side door is circled. *National Archives via James Noblin*

USS *Cetus* (AK-77) was another Liberty ship that the US Navy acquired. Originally named SS *George B. Cortelyou,* it was constructed by Permanente Metals at Richmond, California. The ship is shown in a January 5, 1943, photo at San Francisco before it underwent conversion to US Navy standards. *National Archives via James Noblin*

The photographer set up his camera off the port stern of USS *Cetus* for this view on January 5, 1943. The mizzenmast lacked a crow's nest, but one would be installed on it within the next week or so. The ship also would get a 5-inch/38-caliber dual-purpose gun and two 20 mm antiaircraft guns on the platform atop the after deckhouse in the next few days. *National Archives via James Noblin*

USS *Cetus* is underway on January 12, 1943, following modifications to bring it up to US Navy standards for a cargo ship. Since the January 5 photos of the ship were taken, not only had antiaircraft guns been installed atop the after deckhouse; two tubs for 20 mm antiaircraft guns had been added to the rear of the top of the house to supplement the two tubs already at the front of that level. Conversion work on Liberty ships was done speedily at San Francisco. *National Archives via James Noblin*

USS *Cetus* is underway off San Francisco on January 12, 1943. Like the Liberty ships USS *Cassiopeia*, USS *Celeno*, and USS *Carina*, covered above, the *Cetus*'s first assignment would be to the Solomon Islands in the South Pacific, where the United States was in a monumental struggle to wrest control of the area from the Japanese. *National Archives via James Noblin*

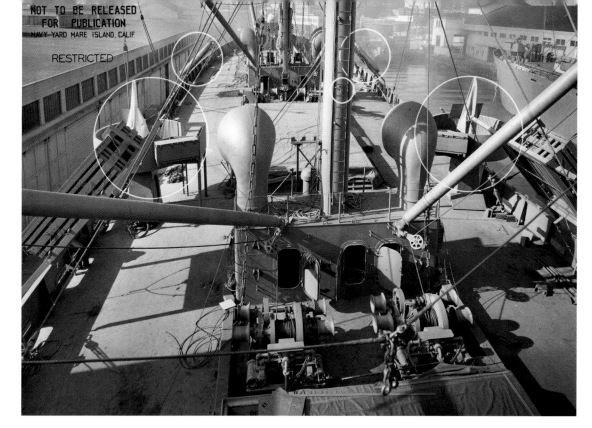

The forward part of USS *Cetus* (AK-77) is viewed from the top of the house in a January 17, 1943, photo at San Francisco. On the main deck in the foreground are two winches and the mainmast locker, with three doors on its aft side. The aft booms of the mainmast are mounted on swivel-type brackets on the rear of the locker. Note the ladder on the rear of the mainmast. *National Archives via James Noblin*

USS *Celeno* (AK-76) is underway at low speed off Mare Island Navy Yard, California, on November 27, 1943, after returning from duty in the Solomon Islands and undergoing some alterations. Without a cargo complement aboard, the ship is riding high, far above its waterline when loaded. *National Archives via James Noblin*

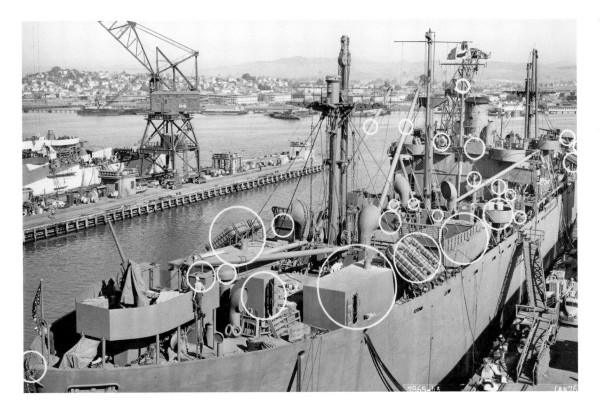

While delivering cargo to Guadalcanal on June 16, 1943, USS *Celeno* (AK-76) was attacked by Japanese bombers, suffering damage and the loss of fifteen crewmen killed and nineteen wounded. After temporary repairs at Espiritu Santo, the ship returned to the Bay Area and received more repairs as well as modifications at Mare Island Navy Yard. In this overhead view from off the port bow looking aft on November 26, 1943, the new changes and special cargoes are indicated by circles. Balsa life rafts had replaced the wooden life rafts. A hatch cover and an unidentified structure with a roof vent are just aft of the 3-inch antiaircraft gun platform on the forecastle. *National Archives via James Noblin*

A cage-type locker has been installed on the boat deck to the port side of the skylights of USS *Celeno* in this view from amidships looking forward. On the port side of the main deck between the superstructure and the forward life-raft rack is a landing craft, mechanized (LCM), secured for transport. *National Archives via James Noblin*

USS *Celeno* is viewed from the front of the port side of the superstructure, facing aft, on November 26, 1943. A searchlight and platform have been added to the front of the top of the house, to the left of the photo. Stowed on the deck between the aft lifeboat and the life-raft rack is a landing craft, vehicle, personnel (LCVP). *National Archives via James Noblin*

A convoy of transport ships, including a Liberty ship in the foreground, proceed with vital supplies and equipment for the Allied fighting forces during World War II. Rushed into development and production to meet the exigencies of the war, the Liberty ships proved vital in the massive logistical efforts that helped win that war. *National Archives*

The nearly new SS *Rufus King*, laden with medical equipment and aircraft, ran aground off Amity Bar near Moreton Island, Queensland. On July 7, 1942, the ship broke in two. The forward section was salvaged and refloated by the Commonwealth Marine Salvage Board. The bow was transferred to the US Army Small Ships Section, which fitted it with a vertical boiler to operate an onboard machine shop, as well as coal and oil bunkers. Serving as a repair-and-service barge fittingly named *Rufus Half* and giving the number S-129, the vessel operated in Milne Bay and later Finschafen. *Rufus King* had been built by California Shipbuilding and launched in March 1942. *National Archives*

SS *James Randall*, Maritime Commission hull number 979, is viewed off its port stern in a photo taken sometime between April and June 1943. A number of large shipping containers are stored on the deck and on the cargo hatches. The life rafts are of a pontoon type, constituting a platform on two long cylinders. Bedding is hanging over the gunwale at the stern for drying out. *National Archives via Rick Davis*

At 0400 on June 10, 1944 while lying at anchor off Utah Beach, Liberty ship *Charles Morgan* was hit in hatch 5 by a 500-pound German bomb. The blast opened the portside shell plating from the number 4 hold to the steering engine room, killing one crewman and seven soldiers aboard. *National Archives*

Charles Morgan settled until its stern was on the bottom and its bow was afloat. The crew abandoned ship, but an effort was made to salvage the vessel, as seen here with USS LCT-474 and a fleet tug (ATF) alongside. Ultimately, the ship, which had been built by Houston Shipbuilding, was written off as a total loss. *National Archives*

SS *Robert Rowan* blazes after being attacked by Nazi aircraft off Gela during the Sicily invasion. The ship was built by North Carolina Shipbuilding in Wilmington and launched April 6, 1943. Operating in the Mediterranean, it arrived at Gela on July 11, 1943, laden with 334 soldiers of the 18th Infantry Regiment, forty-one crewmen and thirty-two US Navy guards, and 2,900 tons of ammunition. Just before 1400 the ship was hit by three 1,000-pound bombs dropped by Luftwaffe Junkers Ju 88 bombers, setting the vessel afire. *National Archives*

Knowing the nature of the cargo, the captain immediately ordered the ship abandoned. Remarkably, everyone aboard successfully got off before the fire reached the ammunition and the ship exploded, less than an hour after the first bomb landed. *National Archives*

Soldiers quickly unload a Liberty ship tied up at Naples on October 7, 1943. Virtually every bullet, gun, shoe, truck, or tank was brought into the combat theater in the hold or on the deck of a Liberty ship. *National Archives*

Several hundred Liberty ships were assigned to the War Shipping Administration (WSA), an emergency war agency established on February 7, 1942. Once the WSA was established, it acted as the United States' ship-operating agency, while the Maritime Commission acted as the shipbuilding agency. Ships serving under the WSA were assigned numbers prefixed by WSAT, the letter *T* standing for transport. One example was the troopship SS *Eugene Hale* (WSAT-550), seen here in a December 1943 photograph. *National Archives via Rick Davis*

Liberty ships sometimes were equipped with torpedo nets, which were rigged on special, extra-long booms and lowered into the water to detonate torpedoes at a safe distance from the hull. SS *James A. Farrell*, Maritime Commission hull number 1016, is shown rigged with torpedo nets to the sides of the mizzenmast. Ironically, the *Farrell* was torpedoed in the English Channel in 1944 and subsequently was scrapped. *National Archives via Rick Davis*

Another Liberty ship that was transferred to the War Shipping Administration was the SS *Elijah White*, built by the Oregon Shipbuilding Corporation, Portland, Oregon. When this ship was photographed in April 1944, it had torpedo nets rigged on the special, long booms. The ship is shown transporting eight Lockheed P-38s with the outer wing sections and the rudders removed. *National Archives via Rick Davis*

SS *Joseph Warren*, Maritime Commission hull number 782, was laid down on February 1, 1943, and launched two months later, on April 5. It was the first Liberty ship launched at the South Portland, Maine, yard of New England Shipbuilding Corporation, commonly known as New England Ship. After the war, the *Joseph Warren* was sold to a private concern in 1947 and was scrapped in 1969. Note the fully enclosed auxiliary bridge on the house top, and the cargo of dozens of US half-tracks on the main deck. *National Archives via Rick Davis*

Three Liberty ships ride at anchor in Manila harbor, Philippines, in August 1945. Barges BKC-35 (*left*) and BKC-27-6 (*right*) are tied to the nearest, the SS *Jerry S. Foley*. *Foley* was completed by St. Johns River Shipbuilding, Jacksonville, Florida, in October 1944. In the foreground, the smokestack of a sunken Japanese cargo ship protrudes above the waves, its peeling paint revealing traces of prewar shipping-line funnel markings. *National Archives*

Under the watchful eye of French longshoremen, German prisoners of war unload coal from the SS *Conrad Kohrs* at Marseille. *National Archives*

A 2-8-2 wheel arrangement steam locomotive is lifted from the SS *Harold O. Wilson* in November 1945. The locomotive, being brought ashore at Marseille, is one of almost 700 that the freighters brought to the war-ravaged nation to aid in rebuilding the infrastructure. *National Archives*

Just as the Liberty ships had carried GIs and their gear to the far corners of the world, they would bring the troops back home. Here, GIs board a Liberty ship (*right*) and a C4 cargo ship (the largest type of cargo ship built by the US Maritime Commission during World War II) in Le Havre, France, on July 11, 1945. *National Archives*

Its decks crowded with troops, SS *Carlos Carrillo* steams into San Francisco Bay just after the war. *Carlos Carrillo* was built as an EC2-S-C1 cargo vessel by California Shipbuilding. It was launched at Terminal Island, California, on January 15, 1943, and immediately converted to a troop carrier. It was broken up in Portland, Oregon, in 1963. *Naval History and Heritage Command*

After World War II, many of the 2,400 surviving Liberty ships were laid up on various maritime reserve fleets around the nation, such as these that were part of the Hudson River Reserve Fleet, shown in June 1946. Many of these ships were reactivated during the Korean War, and many others were sold surplus, rebuilding the commercial shipping industry, which had been devastated by war, especially overseas.

CHAPTER 2
The Liberty Ship Preserved

The 2,710 Liberty ships placed into service between 1941 and 1945 provided a vital link in the supply chain not only of US but also Allied forces during World War II. Although the basic design itself was obsolete even before the first one slid down the builder's ways, it had the advantage of being relatively easy to produce, and simple to operate and maintain. Thus, the vessels were mass-produced by no fewer than eighteen shipyards. Building time, initially 244 days, dropped to forty-two days per ship, although as a publicity stunt the *Robert E. Peary* was launched four days and fifteen and a half hours after the keel was laid.

The welded construction of the ships, combined with the cold of the North Atlantic, led to some cracking in the ships, especially the early ones. In fact, three of the 2,710 ships were lost as a result of these cracks.

While the Liberty ships, with their triple-expansion reciprocating engines and steam winches, were superseded by the larger, more powerful Victory ships, with electric cargo-handling gear, even before the war was over, the Liberty ships labored on for many years. The post–World War II National Defense Reserve Fleet was heavily populated by Liberty ships at eight anchorages. While some were recalled for duty during the Korean War, and some were used for government grain storage during the 1950s, most were sold for commercial use or, in later years, scrapping.

Today, three Liberty ships remain afloat. *Hellas Liberty*, formerly the SS *Arthur M. Huddell*, serves as a museum to the Greek shipping industry in Piraeus Harbor, Greece. Following World War II, the Greek shipping industry was largely rebuilt using surplus Liberty ships, and the *Hellas Liberty* is restored to civil configuration rather than wartime configuration. While beautifully restored, the ship is not operational.

In the United States, two ships are preserved and are documented in the following pages.

The SS *John W. Brown*, berthed in Baltimore Harbor, Maryland, was ordered on May 1, 1941. It was built at the Bethlehem-Fairfield Shipyards in Baltimore, having its keel laid on July 28, 1942. It was launched, along with two other Liberty ships, on September 7, 1942, fifty-four days after the keel laying. Its maiden voyage was transporting ten Sherman tanks, 100 jeeps, 200 motorcycles, two P-40 Warhawks, 748 tons of ammunition, and 280 tons of canned pork, all bound for the Soviet Union from ports in the Persian Gulf.

Upon its return to the US, it was the first of 220 Liberty ships to be converted to a Limited Capacity Troopship. This work was done at Bethlehem Shipbuilding's Hoboken, New Jersey, facility. Thereafter the *Brown* would carry a mixture of troops and equipment—and sometimes prisoners of war (POWs). It carried troops taking part in the landings at Anzio and later the invasion of southern France. In total, *John W. Brown* made eight wartime voyages and, following the war, made five more trips carrying occupation troops, coal, grain, and other necessities.

In August 1946, the Maritime Commission entered into an agreement with New York City whereby the *John W. Brown* would be loaned to the city for use as a high school for students interested in seafaring careers. The school operated until 1982, although the *Brown* did not sail as part of the program.

When efforts to preserve the ship locally failed, the *John W. Brown* was towed to Virginia, becoming part of the James River Reserve Fleet. In 1988, the preservationist group "Project Liberty Ship" secured a berth in Baltimore for the ship, and arrangements were made to have it towed to the new location. After a three-year restoration, the vessel began operation as a museum and also began steaming under its own power again.

On the West Coast of the United States is moored the *Jeremiah O'Brien*. Built in South Portland, Maine, by New England Shipbuilding Corporation, it was launched on June 19, 1943, just fifty-six days after the keel was laid.

During World War II it made four round-trip crossings of the Atlantic and notably took part in the Normandy invasion, making eleven crossings of the English Channel, before shifting to the Pacific and steaming to Australia, China, New Guinea, and the Philippines.

Its military service over, on July 2 1946, *Jeremiah O'Brien* was placed in reserve and made part of the Suisun Bay Reserve Fleet, where it remained until 1979. At that time, the National Liberty Ship Memorial acquired the ship and, remarkably, was able to get it underway under its own power on October 6, 1979. The ship was steamed to the Bethlehem Steel Shipyard in San Francisco, to be drydocked for further repair and restoration.

On May 21, 1980, *Jeremiah O'Brien* left the shipyard sailing on its first Annual Seamen's Memorial Cruise, ending the day by tying up at Pier 3 East in the Golden Gate National Recreation Area.

The port bow of the SS *John W. Brown* is displayed. Two stockless bower anchors are visible, their shanks disappearing up the hawsepipes. The small numbers on the hull are draft marks, indicating the distance to the bottom of the keel in feet.

Although it is often said that Liberty ships were of all-welded construction, this was not always the case. In this photo of the bow of the *Jeremiah O'Brien*, the plates of the shell, or outer skin of the hull, were welded together and riveted to the frame of the ship.

SS *Jeremiah O'Brien* is viewed from its bow, docked at its permanent berth at Pier 45, at the foot of Taylor Street, San Francisco, California. The ship was constructed at the New England Shipbuilding Corporation, South Portland, Maine, and was launched on June 19, 1943. The *Jeremiah O'Brien* is the only remaining ship of the vast Allied naval force that participated in the D-day landings in Normandy on June 6, 1944, and on the fiftieth anniversary of those landings, the ship returned to Normandy. The *O'Brien* has been on display at San Francisco since 1979 and serves as the National Liberty Ship Memorial.

The forecastle of SS *Jeremiah O'Brien* is viewed from the port side. Mounted on the top of the bow are a small davit (*to the left*) and the jackstaff (*to the right*). To the top right is the bulwark of the forward gun tub; below it are tubular supports for the tub.

A close-up view of the forecastle of the *Jeremiah O'Brien* shows the design of the bulwarks, rails, and frame members in this area and the lower parts of the davit and the jackstaff. Cleats are visible on the rail, the davit, and the jackstaff.

The details of the forecastle of the SS *John W. Brown* are similar to those of the *Jeremiah O'Brien*. On either side are roller chocks, through which mooring lines pass. The rollers reduced the wear and tear on the lines that conventional chocks would cause.

Mooring lines are belayed around the double bitt in the left foreground. To the left is a hatch leading down to the boatswain's stores, on a flat between the main, or upper, deck and the second deck. The second deck is the first full deck below the main deck.

At the center is the port hawsepipe, through which the anchor chain passes to the anchor. The hawsepipes of Liberty ships were designed by W. G. Esmond. Attached to the anchor at the lower left is a stopper, a safety measure that immobilized the chain.

The hawsepipes have a detachable cover, to prevent men from falling into the opening. Three dogs, or toggling screw latches, are lying loose. To lock down the cover, the dogs are raised and the wing nuts are tightened onto the cover.

A full view is provided of a stopper. To the front of the stopper is a hook called the devil's claw, which is attached to the chain; the other end of the stopper is attached with a clevis to a pad eye on the deck. In between is a turnbuckle, for tightening the stopper.

The windlass, the engine that raises and lowers the anchor, is on the forecastle. Two drums, called wildcats, grasp the links of the anchor chain and cause them to move. The windlass is equipped with a braking mechanism, allowing it to pay out the chain.

The windlass is viewed from the port side. On the side of the windlass is a warping head, for pulling hawsers during docking operations. To the left is a small deckhouse with a door facing the windlass; this deckhouse helps support the gun tub above it.

The windlass on the SS *John W. Brown* is viewed from aft. From the rear of the wildcats, the two anchor chains pass down through chain pipes to the chain locker belowdecks. The design of the framework on the underside of the forward gun tub is visible.

The windlass on the *Jeremiah O'Brien* is viewed from the starboard side. Liberty ship windlasses were two-cylinder, steam-driven mechanisms and were able to simultaneously lift two anchors from a depth of 30 fathoms at a rate of 30 feet per second.

The starboard anchor chain on the SS *Jeremiah O'Brien* is shown as it passes by the small deckhouse. These chains were formed of forged or cast steel in 15-fathom lengths; these lengths were connected together with patented oval, detachable links.

The forward gun tub and platform of the *John W. Brown* are viewed from the aft port quarter on the forecastle. In the foreground on the platform is a winch. To the right is a ship's bell, and to the left is a catwalk connecting to the port 20 mm gun tub.

Looking aft from the port side of the *John W. Brown*'s forecastle, the catwalk seen in the preceding photo is again in view. The port forward 20 mm gun tub is protected with plastic armor, molded from Trinidad asphalt and crushed stone, about 5 inches thick.

As can be seen in this view from the port side of the forecastle of the SS *Jeremiah O'Brien*, this Liberty ship did not have the tubs for the 20 mm antiaircraft guns in this area, as did the SS *John W. Brown*. Two cowl vents are at the center of the photo.

Specifications	
Displacement:	14,245 long tons
Length:	441 ft., 6 in.
Beam:	56 ft., 10.75 in.
Draft:	27 ft., 9.25 in.
Propulsion:	Two oil-fired boilers
	Triple-expansion steam engine
	Single screw, 2,500 horsepower
Speed:	11–11.5 knots
Range:	20,000 nautical miles
Capacity:	10,856 tons deadweight
Complement:	38–60 US Merchant Marines
	20–41 US Navy Armed Guards
Armament:	Stern-mounted 4- or 5-inch deck gun for use against surfaced submarines; a variety of antiaircraft guns

From the starboard side of the forecastle of the *Jeremiah O'Brien*, facing aft, in the foreground is a fairlead in the form of a roller on a pedestal, used in routing a hawser from the warping head around obstructions while protecting the hawser from chafing.

On the lower front of the forward gun tub on the SS *Jeremiah O'Brien* is a ship's bell. The bell was rung to announce the time during a four-hour watch. There were eight bells rung during each watch: one every half hour. The bell also was rung in foggy weather.

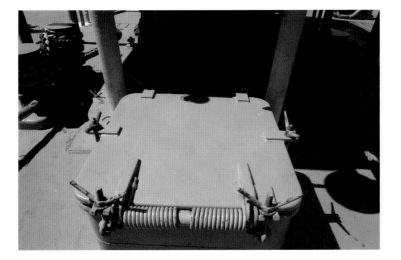

This hatch on the forecastle of the SS *Jeremiah O'Brien* leads down to the boatswain's stores and is located forward of the tubular supports below the front of the forward gun tub. The hatch cover is locked shut with six dogs; the coil spring is a lift assist.

The air scoop of a cowl ventilator on the foredeck of the *Jeremiah O'Brien* is shown. A screen is fitted over the opening, to keep out insects and foreign objects. The green sheeting in the background is the cover fitted over the hatch above hold number 1.

This single, pedestal-mounted 3-inch/50-caliber gun is in the forward gun platform of the SS *Jeremiah O'Brien*. Originally, there were two such guns on this ship. The Liberty ships' defensive weapons were tended by members of the Naval Armed Guard.

The front of the pedestal, or carriage, of the 3-inch/50-caliber gun mount is depicted. The entire carriage turned when the gun was trained, or traversed. Visible below the recoil cylinder on the bottom of the gun is the front of the elevating arc.

Affixed to the base of the pedestal of the 3-inch/50-caliber gun is a platform for the sight setter to stand on. The seat to the front of the platform was for the pointer, who controlled the elevation of the piece. The breech of the gun is to the upper right.

The rear of the gun is seen from the port side, showing the side of the curved, brass-colored elevation indicator. The round fixture at the center is the elevation drum; the fitting with the knurled knob above it is the azimuth drum. To the left is the port trunnion.

Attached to a yoke over the gun is the pointer's ring-and-bead sight, above which is a sight guard. At the lower center is also a mount for the pointer's telescope. This type of gun required a crew of at least eleven men to properly serve it.

The 3-inch/50-caliber gun had a range against surface targets of 14,600 yards and a maximum range ceiling of 29,400 feet against aerial targets. Its muzzle velocity was 2,700 feet per second. The barrel is approximately 150 inches long.

The SS *Jeremiah O'Brien*'s 3-inch/50-caliber gun is viewed from the starboard side, showing the trainer's seat and training handwheel, by which the trainer manually traversed the gun mount. Above the hand wheel is the trainer's ring-and-bead sight, which is fitted with a cushioned rubber eyepiece. The gun barrel fits in the slide, a cylindrical assembly with trunnions that serves to hold the gun barrel, permitting it to elevate as well as to recoil and recuperate. The side of the slide is visible in the left half of the photo. The smaller cylinder next to it (*to the left*) is the operating-spring case. *Richard Thresh*

Liberty ships were designed with a foremast at frame 39, a mainmast at frame 68, and a mizzenmast at frame 134. The main purpose of the masts on a Liberty ship was to support the cargo booms. As originally designed, four 5-ton booms and one 30-ton boom were mounted around the foremast, two 5-ton booms were mounted abeam the mainmast, and four 5-ton booms and one 15-ton boom were mounted adjacent to the mizzenmast. The 5-ton booms had a working angle of 25 degrees, while the 15- and 30-ton booms had a working angle of 35 degrees. In this photo, the foremast and booms of the SS *John W. Brown* are shown.

The foremast of the SS *Jeremiah O'Brien* is viewed from the forward gun platform, facing aft. Tilting booms are arrayed around the foremast as well as around the mainmast in the background. In the left foreground is the front of a cowl ventilator.

At the top of the foremast of the *Jeremiah O'Brien* is a crow's nest, and painted on it is a cartoon of Bruce D. Raven, a character in *Farley*, a comic strip by Phil Frank that sometimes featured the *Jeremiah O'Brien*. The late Mr. Frank painted this artwork.

The foremast and booms of the *Jeremiah O'Brien* are displayed. The bases of the booms are attached to fittings on the boat locker: the deckhouse around the base of the mast. The fittings for the 5-ton booms were strong enough to accept 10-ton booms if required.

In front of the mast locker, the deckhouse around the *O'Brien*'s foremast, are two cargo winches, and to each side is a raised platform for a 20 mm antiaircraft cannon. The cannons are present but are under covers. In the left distance is the Golden Gate Bridge.

In the foreground is the foremast of the SS *John W. Brown*. Two 5-ton booms are standing upright and are secured to the top of the mast. Partially hidden behind the mast is a high-capacity "jumbo" boom, the top of which is above and aft of the crow's nest.

The *John W. Brown*'s foremast and booms are viewed from the starboard side. On Liberty ships, the boom to the rear of the foremast (*left*) originally was 30-ton capacity; later, on some Liberty ships, a 50-ton boom was retrofitted in this position.

The foremast locker of the SS *John W. Brown* is viewed from its aft port quarter. A door into the locker is partially hidden behind the large block (pulley) toward the lower left. Above the large block is a smaller block, called a heel block, mounted at the bottom of a 5-ton boom. The bottom of the boom, called the heel, is mounted to a swivel-type bracket called the gooseneck, which is attached to the upper part of the mast locker. The foremast is behind that 5-ton boom. The high-capacity "jumbo" boom standing vertically at the center of the photo is mounted on a different design of fixture.

The foremast locker of the *John W. Brown* is viewed from a closer perspective, showing the port aft heel block. Silhouetted on the opposite corner of the locker is the starboard aft heel block. Two large cowl ventilators are positioned on top of the foremast locker.

The mounting for the high-capacity boom is displayed close-up. This is called a pedestal-type fitting. A reinforced bracket is fastened on top of a pedestal, and in the bracket is fitted a gooseneck, to which the bottom of the boom is attached with a large bolt and nut.

The upper part of the aft port corner of the foremast locker of the SS *John W. Brown* is observed close-up, providing a glimpse of the heel block (*upper center*) and gooseneck for the aft port 5-ton boom. A cable is belayed around a cleat to the left of the gooseneck.

This is the aft port corner of the SS *Jeremiah O'Brien*'s foremast locker, showing, in the background, the design of the mount for the jumbo boom. Several grades of jumbo booms were used on Liberty ships, rated at 15 tons, 30 tons, or 50 tons.

The aft starboard corner of the *John W. Brown*'s foremast locker is shown. The diamond-tread walkways running around the locker are mounted above steam pipes routed to the steam-powered winches. To the upper left is a cargo hook suspended from a boom.

The winch to the aft starboard side of the foremast locker is viewed facing to port, with the starboard winch partially visible in the background. Liberty ships had ten double-geared, steam-driven winches on the main deck, four of which are around the foremast.

The cargo winch aft of the port side of the foremast locker is viewed facing forward. At the center of the winch is the winch drum, with cable wound around it. Projecting from each side of the winch is a vertically mounted capstan, used for hauling on lines, such as the bull ropes used for topping the booms ("topping" meaning lifting the booms into the desired angle). At the bottom of the photo is the forward port corner of the hatch for hold number 2. To the left is a hatch leading down to "tween deck," as the second deck was called.

Winches mounted on the main deck pulled and paid out the cables that operated the booms. At the bottom is a diamond-tread guard over steam pipes, and to the right, a cage has been constructed around a vertical steam pipe as a safety measure; these pipes got hot!

This winch is aft of the port side of the foremast locker on SS *Jeremiah O'Brien* and was manufactured by the American Hoist & Derrick Company, St. Paul, Minnesota.

The forward port 20 mm gun tub on the *John W. Brown* is viewed from aft. The plastic armor on the tub, composed of asphalt and crushed stone, is cracked and sagging in places. To the right of the base of the tub's support pylon is the breakwater.

Jamming was a recurring problem with the 20 mm cannons, and when a round jammed, the barrel was removed and placed in a water-filled tube, such as this one on the forward port tub on SS *John W. Brown*, to cool down so the round could be extracted later.

As can be seen in this photo of the *Jeremiah O'Brien*, this ship's forward 20 mm gun tubs, visible to the left and right, were positioned farther aft than those on the *John W. Brown* and were abeam and slightly forward of the foremast, seen at the center of this photo.

The forward 20 mm gun tubs of the SS *Jeremiah O'Brien* were also of a different design than those of the *John W. Brown*, featuring a box-shaped pedestal. On the right of the gun tub is an access ladder. The sloping structure in the foreground is a hatchway.

The *Jeremiah O'Brien*'s forward port 20 mm gun tub is viewed from the ship's forward 3-inch gun platform. Two barrel-cooling tubes are mounted diagonally on the outside of the tub. The 20 mm gun is covered, but the right side of the gun shield is in view.

The port forward 20 mm gun tub on the *Jeremiah O'Brien* is viewed from the main-deck level, facing aft. The plastic armor on the side of the tub is in a good state of preservation. This unique armor protected the gun crew without the extra weight of steel armor.

SS *Jeremiah O'Brien*'s starboard forward 20 mm gun tub is seen from the forward gun platform. The Liberty ships' 20 mm cannons had a rate of fire of 450 rounds per minute, but this was limited by how quickly the loaders could reload the sixty-round magazines.

In addition to four lifeboats stored on the boat deck of the superstructure, Liberty ships carried a number of life rafts, such as this one, viewed from its aft side, aboard the SS *Jeremiah O'Brien*. It is on a rack attached to the bulwark and the mainsail locker. To deploy the rafts, they were simply released from their racks and fell into the water. To the right is the mainmast, with the mainmast locker below it. Only two booms, 5-ton models, were mounted by the mainmast; the port one rises diagonally in the foreground.

The forward port life raft and stowage rack on the SS *Jeremiah O'Brien* are viewed from another angle. Mounted on the bottom of the 5-ton boom, near the top of the photo, is a fairlead, the purpose of which was to guide the hoist cable. A cowl vent is to the right.

A view from amidships forward on the main deck shows the structure of the life-raft rack. Below the raft, in the background, is the port forward 20 mm gun tub. To the far right, aft of the mainmast locker, is one of two side-by-side steam-powered cargo winches.

This view is a continuation of the preceding one, facing more to the starboard on the main deck of the *Jeremiah O'Brien*, showing the mainmast locker. A ladder runs up the rear of the mast. The green cover to the far left is on the hatch for hold number 3.

The two steam-powered cargo winches that served the two 5-ton booms mounted alongside the mainmast on the SS *Jeremiah O'Brien* are viewed from the port side. Two capstans protrude from each side of each winch. Steam pipes and valves are in evidence.

Unlike the *Jeremiah O'Brien*, the SS *John W. Brown* has this structure, a troop head, or latrine, forward of the mainmast locker. It was installed when the *Brown* was refitted as a troopship. A spare anchor is stowed there. In the background is the superstructure.

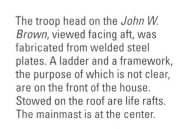

The troop head on the *John W. Brown*, viewed facing aft, was fabricated from welded steel plates. A ladder and a framework, the purpose of which is not clear, are on the front of the house. Stowed on the roof are life rafts. The mainmast is at the center.

Most of the mainmast is visible in this view from the superstructure of SS *John W. Brown*, facing forward. In the foreground are the two steam-powered cargo winches for the two 5-ton booms mounted on the aft side of the mainmast locker. Forward of the winches is the mainmast locker, with two doors on the rear side. Abutting the front of the mainmast locker is the troop head, which is somewhat higher and wider than the mainmast locker. The bow of the ship is in the distance.

The upper part of the mainmast of the *John W. Brown* is observed from high up in the superstructure, facing forward. A ladder consisting of thirty-nine rungs extends up the rear of the mast. At the top of the mainmast is the maintop, a platform with a guardrail around it. On the outer edges of the maintop are two blocks. These are intended to handle the cables of the topping rigging, by which the angles of the booms are regulated. Below the maintop, mounted on brackets protruding from the mainmast, are two spotlights.

The lower section of the mainmast of the *John W. Brown* is observed from the forward port corner of the troop head. Fastened to the bottom of the foretop are shrouds, two on each side, which help steady the mast. The bottoms of the guys are fastened to the deck.

The upper part of the mainmast of the SS *Jeremiah O'Brien*, as viewed from the wheelhouse, is very similar to that of the SS *John W. Brown*, although the *O'Brien*'s maintop lacks a guardrail around it. The form at the top center is the ship's bell.

In a view taken from the forward starboard part of the boat deck of SS *John W. Brown*, facing forward, details of the rear of the mainmast locker are in view, including the goosenecks for the two 5-ton booms and the heel blocks immediately below them. On the roof of the locker, a fixed, aft-facing ventilator is between the cowl ventilators. In the foreground are the hatch cover for hold number 3 and the two cargo winches for the 5-ton booms. Just beyond the mainsail locker is the troop head; to the far right is a door into this compartment.

The rear of SS *John W. Brown*'s mainsail locker is seen from the port side of the main deck. The cowl ventilators are adjustable and have grab handles so crewmen can manually position them to take advantage of the wind or avoid taking in rain or water.

Rising above the mainmast and the maintop on the SS *Jeremiah O'Brien* is the main topmast. On the aft edge of the maintop are clamps for holding the 5-ton booms when stored in the raised position. A topping block is on each side of the maintop.

The front of the superstructure, usually called the midships house, or simply the house, of the SS *John W. Brown* is shown. A key feature of Liberty ships was the inclusion of a single house amidships, rather than multiple houses, since it was thought that one house in this section of the ship would result in drier crew quarters and would economize on heating and piping systems. The navigation bridge is on the third level; three windows at the center of the house mark the location. Plastic armor is present on the front of the bridge. Wing bridges extended from each side on this level. On the roof of the house, above the navigation bridge, are two 20 mm gun tubs and, at the center, the flying bridge, nicknamed "monkey island." The flying bridge functioned as an auxiliary, open-air bridge. On the second level is the boat deck, and one of the ship's boats is visible to the right of the tall cowl vent.

The house of SS *John W. Brown* is observed from its forward starboard quarter. The front of the bridge was constructed of ¼-inch steel with a 5-to-6-inch-thick layer of plastic armor over it. Here, the plastic armor is held in place by disk-shaped retainers.

On Liberty ships, steam-powered cargo winches were mounted on the main deck to the front or the rear of each cargo hatch. This example is on the forward starboard end of the second cargo hatch of *John W. Brown*, showing the starboard front of the house in the background.

The cargo winch to the port side of the one in the preceding photo is depicted. On the inboard side of the winch, attached to the winch drums, are two gypsy heads. These are similar to capstans except that they revolve on a horizontal axis.

The port cargo winch for the second cargo hatch on SS *John W. Brown* is seen in closer detail. Cables from the cargo winches were rigged to the booms in order to lift or lower cargo in the cargo holds. The gypsy heads for the starboard winch are to the upper right.

Two cargo winches on the main deck to the forward end of the second cargo hatch of a Liberty ship are observed from the upper part of the house. To the front of the winches are the mainsail locker, showing the lower part of the mainmast and two cowl ventilators.

To the left side of monkey island atop the front of the house is the flag bag, a metal bin holding the ship's signal flags. In the preceding photograph, the front of the flag bag is in view adjacent to the port 20 mm gun tub. Each flag had its own, labeled, spot in the bin.

A number of small mushroom vents are located on the deck atop the house, to provide ventilation for the compartments in the top level of the house. The caps of the vents are painted white. The deck featured an aggregate-composition nonskid surface.

This structure on the port side of the deck atop the house of the *John W. Brown* is the radio antenna trunk. A lead from the ship's radio antennas was connected to the insulator on top of the trunk and was routed from there to the radio room immediately below.

The port side of the house is viewed from aft of the forward port 20 mm gun tub on the deck atop the house. In the foreground are two of the disk-shaped retainers for a section of plastic armor that is no longer present. Two sections of plastic armor remain intact.

Monkey island, the auxiliary bridge on the deck above the wheelhouse, is viewed from the starboard side on the *John W. Brown*. It is situated on a wooden-grate platform and is equipped with a wheel, a binnacle, an engine-order telegraph, other instruments, and a voice tube. The engine-order telegraph is the fixture with the two levers protruding above it, to the right of the wheel, and it served to relay instructions on engine speed and direction to the engine room, signaling changes in engine order with the ringing of a bell and a change in position of an indicator. On the starboard side of the station is a plywood gunwale. *Richard Thresh*

This is monkey island on the SS *Jeremiah O'Brien*. A cover is lashed to the tubular frame around the auxiliary bridge. Covers are fitted over the wheel, binnacle, and engine-order telegraph. This bridge was exposed to the elements but offered good all-around visibility.

The deck on top of the house is viewed from the port side of the smokestack, visible to the left. The flag bag is in view at the center, to the right of which is monkey island, partially hidden by the cowl vent. In the background are the mainmast and foremast.

The forward port 20 mm gun tub on top of the house of SS *John W. Brown* is viewed from aft, showing the texture of the plastic armor and the retaining bands. To the left of the tub is a pelorus stand with gyrocompass repeater and a 12-inch signal lamp.

The inside of the forward port 20 mm gun tub atop the house on SS *Jeremiah O'Brien* is viewed facing forward. The Oerlikon 20 mm gun is fully elevated and is mounted on a tripod stand, with a two-piece armor shield. A sixty-round magazine is fitted on the gun.

The *Jeremiah O'Brien*'s starboard forward 20 mm gun tub on top of the house is seen from the rear. To the left is an access ladder for the tub. To the far right is the starboard pelorus stand. To the right of the gun shield is a radar mast apparently installed after World War II.

Running around part of the inner perimeter of the gun tubs on top of the *Jeremiah O'Brien*'s 20 mm gun tubs are curved steps made of diamond-tread steel. The base of the postwar radar mast is to the right of the gun mount. San Francisco is in the background.

Projecting through the deck on top of the house is the smokestack. The smokestack of the Liberty ships, in this case the SS *John W. Brown*, was a fairly simple assembly on the outside, with an access ladder on the rear. Several lockers are in the foreground.

The stack of the SS *John W. Brown*, viewed here from the forward port side of the deck, with the port 20 mm gun tub to the left. Monkey island is to the far left, and four large cowl ventilators are arranged around the smokestack.

The *John W. Brown*'s smokestack is observed close-up from its port aft quarter. Attached to the stack are a number of stays intended to brace the smokestack from the effects of wind and rough seas. To the left is the radio mast, equipped with ladder rungs.

The SS *Jeremiah O'Brien*'s smokestack is viewed, showing how the stays are fastened to pad eyes welded to a ring around the stack. The ship's steam whistle is adjacent to the top of the ladder. Below the whistle is a small work platform with diagonal braces.

A close-up view of the steam whistle on the *Jeremiah O'Brien* shows how the steam pipe exits from the smokestack and enters the bottom of the whistle. A ladder-shaped bracket holds the top of the whistle, while a more substantial bracket holds the bottom.

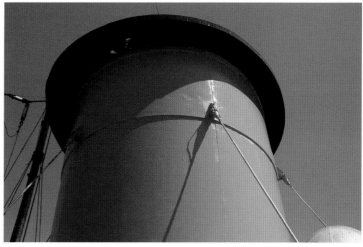

The whistle on the front of the *O'Brien*'s smokestack is viewed from the port side. The oval shape in the foreground is the opening of a cowl vent, covered with a screen. To the right is the small mast seen in the preceding photo beyond the steam whistle.

The SS *Jeremiah O'Brien*'s smokestack is viewed from the rear, showing details of the stays and the welded construction. The cap at the top of the smokestack has suffered some deterioration, and daylight is visible through several holes in it.

The port side of the deck atop of the house of SS *John W. Brown* is viewed facing forward. The large cowl vents were too big to be rotated manually, so they were fitted with ring gears and a hand-cranked pinion, as seen on the second vent on the right.

In a photo taken from inside the aft port gun tub on top of the house of the *Brown*, a sixty-round 20 mm ammunition magazine is displayed on a ready-magazine holder. The magazine lies on its rear; the handgrip made it easier to handle the heavy magazine.

On a board affixed to the starboard rails on top of the house of the *O'Brien* are campaign ribbons for the operations the ship participated in during World War II. In the background is the aft starboard 20 mm gun tub; to the right is a 20 mm ready-service ammunition locker.

The SS *Jeremiah O'Brien*'s aft starboard 20 mm gun tub on the deck atop the house is viewed close-up, facing aft. The access ladder offered the crew the means of entering or egressing from the tub. Diagonally mounted 20 mm barrel-cooling tubes are next to the ladder. The defensive guns of the Liberty ships were manned by members of the Naval Armed Guard, who were members of the US Navy, rather than the Merchant Marine, who made up the crew that operated the ship. Typically, forty-one members of the Naval Armed Guard were assigned to each Liberty ship.

The aft port 20 mm cannon and gun tub on the SS *Jeremiah O'Brien* are depicted. In the foreground next to the access ladder are gun-barrel cooling tubes. The armor shields on the gun mount are fastened to V-shaped brackets. A magazine is fitted onto the gun.

Loaded sixty-round magazines for the 20 mm cannons were stored in ready-service lockers such as this one. The removable cover is secured in place with dogs: swiveling bolts with large ring nuts that are snugged down onto catches welded to the cover.

This view was taken at the top of the ladder leading to the starboard wing bridge on the *John W. Brown*. The wing bridges are open-air platforms extending from each side of the wheelhouse. A small spotlight is mounted on the rail at the rear of the wing bridge.

A spotlight similar to the one in the preceding photo is shown on the *Jeremiah O'Brien*. Such a light would have been used to illuminate an area for the benefit of the deck crew when necessary; its use while at sea was restricted due to the U-boat threat.

Several pieces of equipment are fastened to the deck in the forward starboard extension of the boat deck of the *Jeremiah O'Brien*, including a small electrically powered winch to the right. A deck chair is present, and in the background is the main deck.

The same section of the forward extension of the boat deck illustrated in the preceding photo is shown from a different perspective. The vertical posts to the right of center form stanchions for the guardrails and also help support the wing bridge above.

The main deck of the SS *Jeremiah O'Brien* is observed from the forward starboard extension of the boat deck. In the foreground are two cowl ventilators that are mounted on the main deck. In the right background is the forward starboard 20 mm gun tub.

This ladder on the starboard side of the house of the *John W. Brown* leads up to the top deck from the wing bridge. Next to the ladder is plastic armor on the side of the house, with some of the disk-shaped retainers being visible. In the foreground is boat number 1.

Boat number 1 of the SS *John W. Brown* is viewed from above. The interior of this motorized vessel is painted orange for high visibility. Manually operated round-bar boat davits were used on Liberty ships instead of mechanical davits, for simplicity's sake.

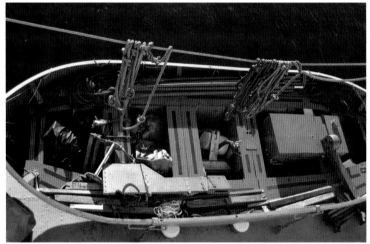

The knotted ropes hanging from the line stretched between the tops of the boat davits are monkey ropes: personnel in the boat could grasp these lines for safety while standing up in the boat as it was being raised or lowered. The rudder is lying on the seats. *Richard Thresh*

The starboard side of the boat deck of the SS *Jeremiah O'Brien*, the first level above the main deck, is viewed from above, facing aft. The boats are fitted with covers. First in line is boat number 1, and aft of it is boat number 3. Boats 2 and 4 are on the port side of the boat deck. Boat number 1 has data on its capacity, twenty-five persons or 297 cubic feet, painted on the side of its bow. The davits are of a type referred to as Liberty ship davits. Similar to but easier to operate than quadrant davits, they were operated by hand cranks that rotated a worm gear in the actuating strut, the smaller-diameter tube inboard of the main arm of the davit.

The lower part of one of the *Jeremiah O'Brien*'s davits is viewed. The main arm of the davit is on a pivot mount on the outboard side of the davit frame. The fittings for the hand cranks that operated the swing of the davit are just above the inboard side of the frame.

In the foreground is a cruciform bitt with a boat-fall line belayed around it. Mounted on the deck aft of the bitt is the fall reel, for stowing the boat-fall line. A cover is fitted over the reel to protect the line from the elements. This boat has a capacity of thirty-one occupants.

The propeller of one of the SS *Jeremiah O'Brien*'s lifeboats is viewed. The boat's rudder is not installed. The rudder was not shipped, or inserted into its mounts, until the boat was being lowered to the water. To the right are a davit frame and hand-crank fitting.

Boat number 1 of the SS *John W. Brown* is viewed from the bow, showing, to the left, part of a davit and the worm-gear strut, as well as details of the rigging of the boat falls. Various sizes of boats were used on Liberty ships; this one could hold twenty-eight crewmen.

The *John W. Brown*'s boat number 1 is viewed from aft. The Liberty ship davit pivoted on the outboard end of the davit frame, with the action of the worm-gear strut pushing the top of the davit outboard, to a position suitable for lowering or raising the boat.

The port side of the boat deck of the SS *Jeremiah O'Brien* is observed from the top of the house, facing aft. A short distance up San Francisco Bay, in the center background, is Sausalito, where the Marinship facility produced fifteen Liberty ships.

Boat number 4 on the aft port corner of the *O'Brien*'s boat deck is fitted with a cover with small openings at the front and rear to accommodate the hooks on the boat-fall blocks. Monkey ropes are suspended from the line attached to the tops of the davits.

SS *Jeremiah O'Brien*'s boat number 4 is viewed from its starboard side, also displaying the davits, boat falls, fall reels, and, partially visible, cruciform bitts. The cable between the tops of the davits, to which the monkey ropes (sometimes called manropes) are attached, is called the span wire. The boat rests on two chocks attached to the boat deck. Adjacent to the chocks are chains that hold the boat in place. These chains are fastened to the boat's gunwales and are fitted with turnbuckles for tightening them.

Boat number 4 on the *John W. Brown* is seen, with the bow to the right. Toward the bottom of the hull are grab rails. These were to be fitted on all Merchant Marine lifeboats and were a means of hanging on to and righting an overturned boat.

Boats numbers 2 and 4 on the port side of the boat deck of SS *John W. Brown* are observed from the forward part of the deck on top of the house. Canvas covers are fitted over these boats. The davits are shown in their normal stowed position. At times when a Liberty ship was operating under emergency conditions, such as when the threat of attack was high, the davits would be turned outward, so the boats could be lowered rapidly. In the background is the aft port 20 mm gun tub on top of the house.

The aft part of the boat deck of the SS *Jeremiah O'Brien* is viewed from the top deck of the house. Numerous cowl ventilators are in view, and farther aft are the aft 5-ton booms and two aft life-raft racks. Note the ring gear on the ventilator at the center.

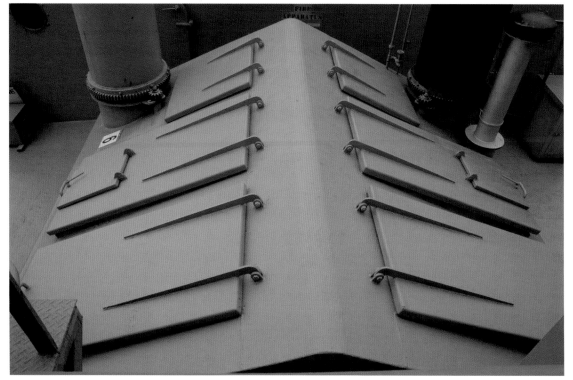

Toward the rear of the boat deck is a skylight with hinged covers, located over the engine room. This view on the *John W. Brown* was taken from a similar position to that in the preceding photo of the *O'Brien*, which lacks the deckhouse seen here in the background.

The skylight on the *Jeremiah O'Brien*'s boat deck is viewed facing forward. The hinged covers on the skylight were operated mechanically from inside the engine room. Two large cowl ventilators are mounted on the rear of the structure. Toward the bottom of the shaft of the closer cowl ventilator is the ring gear for rotating the vent. Several mushroom vents are present on the deck. To the top are the rears of the two aft 20 mm gun tubs atop the house. In the right background is boat number 3. To the far left is a ladder up to the aft end of the bridge deck. The deck chairs are for the convenience of visitors.

The aft port corner of the house of the *John W. Brown* is viewed. This area is designated fire station number 4 and is equipped with a fire plug and hose. The door leads into the port corridor of the officers' quarters, and the ladder leads up to the bridge deck.

This landing is at the rear of the bridge deck on the *Brown*. To the right is a ladder up to the deck on top of the house. Behind the cylindrical post to the right of center is a corridor to officers' quarters on the port side of this level, including the radio operator's.

The same area on the rear of the bridge deck shown in the preceding photo is shown on the SS *Jeremiah O'Brien*. The design of the aft end of the deck is different on each ship. To the upper right is the underside of the aft port 20 mm gun tub on the top deck.

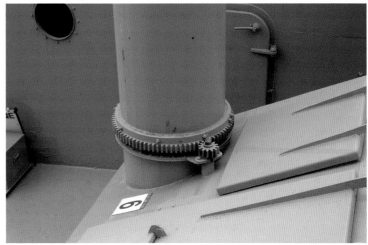

The ring gear on one of the skylight-mounted cowl ventilators on SS *John W. Brown* is shown close-up. The pinion mounted next to the ring gear drove the gear, thus rotating the vent to the desired position. In the background is the auxiliary generator house.

The skylight above the engine room of the *John W. Brown* is viewed from the port side. The arrangement of the cowl vents on the rear of the skylight is similar to that on the *Jeremiah O'Brien*, but the mushroom vent on the tall stack is not present on the *O'Brien*.

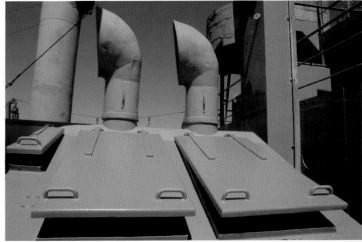

Unlike the skylight on the SS *John W. Brown*, the skylight on the SS *Jeremiah O'Brien* has two small cowl vents mounted on the ridge of the structure. These are equipped with handles for manually turning the vents. Handles are also on the hinged panels.

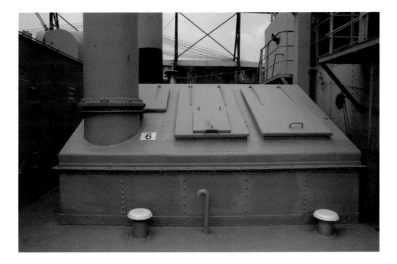

The center starboard hinged panel on the skylight of the *John W. Brown* has a separate, smaller hinged cover toward the bottom. Two mushroom vents with white caps and a gooseneck vent are on the deck adjacent to the skylight.

This deckhouse at the rear of the boat deck of SS *John W. Brown* contained two auxiliary Diesel-powered generators and was added when the ship was converted to a limited-capacity troopship during World War II. This feature is not present on the *O'Brien*.

The rear of the bridge deck of the SS *John W. Brown* is viewed from the port aft corner of the boat deck. The ladder provides access to the corridors running fore and aft through the bridge deck; there is a similar ladder on the starboard side. To the lower right is the skylight. To the left are the two portside 20 mm gun tubs on the deck atop the house. The aft starboard 20 mm gun tub is also visible. Note how the rears of the two aft gun tubs come nearly flush with the rear of the house, with most of their overhangs being over the sides of the house.

In contrast to the SS *John W. Brown*, most of the overhang of the aft 20 mm gun tubs atop the house of SS *Jeremiah O'Brien* is toward the rear, with slight overhangs to the sides of the house. The framing and supports under the tub are illustrated.

The rear of the amidships superstructure of the SS *John W. Brown* is observed from the port side of the main deck, facing forward. Dominating the rear of the boat deck, the second level above the main deck, is the auxiliary generator house, which has a plain surface, interrupted only by two portholes and two small ventilation openings with hinged covers at the lower outer corners. Atop the auxiliary generator house, two mufflers and exhaust pipes for the Diesel engines that power the generators are visible. To the lower right is the cover over the hatch for hold number 4.

The afterdeck, or the main deck aft of the superstructure, of the *John W. Brown* is observed from the port aft corner of the boat deck. To the left of center is the lower part of the mizzenmast, surrounded by booms. Aft of it is the hatch for hold number 5.

The two steam-powered winches forward of the mizzenmast are viewed facing forward, with the ship's house and the hatch cover for hold number 4 in the background. A network of pipes furnished steam to the engines of the winches.

The port cargo winch forward of the mizzenmast locker (*to the right*) is viewed from the side, showing the two vertically oriented capstans on the side, for handling lines. To the rear of the capstans is a cylinder, and a crankshaft is below the capstans.

The same winch on the SS *John W. Brown* seen in the preceding photo is viewed from its aft starboard side, showing the two capstans mounted on that side of the winch. Operating levers are in the left foreground; details of the design of the cable drum are visible.

The starboard side of the afterdeck of SS *John W. Brown* is viewed from above. The structure with the slanted side in the center foreground, just aft of the hatch for hold number 4, is a crew hatchway leading down to the second deck, also known as the tween deck. Next aft are the cargo winches, the cowl ventilators, and the mizzenmast and related cargo booms. To the sides of the cowl ventilators are the aft life-raft racks. Farther aft are gun tubs for defensive weapons. In the distance are the kingposts of another ship docked at the same pier.

With a cowl ventilator to the left, the upper part of the mizzenmast of the SS *Jeremiah O'Brien* is viewed from the front. The vertical "pole" secured to the front of the mizzenmast is a jumbo cargo boom. Next to the top of the boom is the topmast.

A closer view is offered of the top of the jumbo boom secured to the mizzenmast of the *Jeremiah O'Brien*. At the top of the boom is a fixture called the spider, to which are attached guys and blocks for handling the topping rigging and the hoisting rigging.

The upper part of the mizzenmast and its platform on the *John W. Brown* are seen from aft. The mizzen topmast is the thinner mast toward the top. Two clamps on the rear of the platform are for securing booms when raised. On the front of the mast is a jumbo boom.

Partway up the mizzenmast of the SS *John W. Brown*, viewed from the aft port quarter, are four adjustable spotlights, for illuminating the deck for work parties at night. The ladder on the mast is offset to the port side of the longitudinal centerline of the ship.

Viewed from aft on the *John W. Brown* are the platform atop the mizzenmast, the mizzen topmast (*left of center*), and the top of the jumbo boom (*right of center*). Two circular clamps are visible on the rear of the platform, for securing 5-ton booms.

Most of the mizzenmast, as well as the platform and mizzen topmast, of SS *John W. Brown* is viewed from aft. Extending diagonally from around the mast are the four 5-ton booms associated with this mast. Noteworthy is the stepped design of the booms.

The *John W. Brown*'s mizzenmast and related cargo booms are viewed from a different perspective, on the port side of the main deck. A complex array of stays and rigging lines are in view. As is the case with the 5-ton booms associated with the foremast and the mainmast, the 5-inch booms of the mizzenmast are mounted on goosenecks on the upper part of the mast locker. A large cowl ventilator is on each side of the roof of the mizzenmast locker. The locations of the four spotlights partway up the mast are apparent. To the left is a 20 mm gun tub.

The mizzenmast and mizzenmast locker of the SS *John W. Brown* are observed facing forward, with the aft port section of the house and boat deck visible to the left. In the foreground is the hatch cover for hold number 5. Two steam winches between the hatch and the mizzenmast locker serve the two 5-ton booms mounted to the rear of the mizzenmast locker. Two cable drums are on the roof of the locker. Lines are belayed around three cleats near the bottom of the mizzenmast. The ladder running up the mizzenmast and the jumbo boom to the front of the mizzenmast are visible to the left of the mast.

The hatch cover for hold number 5 and the rear of the mizzenmast locker are viewed facing forward. To the starboard sides of these structures are diamond-tread walkways/guards over the steam pipes for the cargo winches.

The two steam-powered cargo winches aft of the mizzenmast on the *John W. Brown* are viewed facing starboard and aft. In the left background on the starboard side of the main deck is one of two 20 mm gun tubs added when the ship was converted to a troopship.

The aft port 20 mm gun tub across the main deck from the tub shown in the preceding photo is viewed facing aft. This gun tub as well as the ones in the background on the fantail lacked plastic armor. Details of the frame and supports for the tub are in view.

The projections with the flat sides on the 20 mm gun tubs were designed to hold a 20 mm ammunition ready-service locker. Placing the guns on high platforms gave them a more unobstructed field of fire.

This view of the aft port 20 mm gun tub on the SS *John W. Brown* is facing forward, with the smokestack visible to the far right. The cover is removed from the 20 mm cannon, showing its barrel, a sixty-round magazine fitted on top of the receiver, a ring-and-bead sight, and shoulder rests. To fire the cannon, the gunner strapped himself to the shoulder rests, so his upper body could control much of the movement of the cannon. At the bottom of the side of the gun tub are thin slots that act as scuppers, to let out water that falls into the tub.
Richard Thresh

In this elevated view of the afterdeck of the SS *John W. Brown*, the aft port 20 mm gun tub is to the left, and part of the starboard aft 20 mm gun tub is visible to the far right. A good view is also provided of the mizzenmast, mizzenmast locker, and cargo booms.

A view similar to the one in the preceding photograph emphasizes the aft starboard 20 mm gun tub on SS *John W. Brown*. At the bottom of the photo is the forward part of the hatch cover for the number 5 hold. The hatch covers over the cargo holds were made of wood, with canvas tarpaulins stretched over them to make them watertight. The cargo hatch covers could be used for lifesaving flotation devices in the event the ship was sunk, provided the crew had time to release the hatch retainers. In actual service, the tarpaulins were held in place by wedges that trapped the edges of the tarpaulin between the hatch coaming and cleats.

The support structure of the starboard aft 20 mm gun tub on the afterdeck of SS *John W. Brown* is illustrated. A large, central pylon with triangular braces supports the framework under the center of the tub, while four stanchions support the outer part of the tub.

In a closer view of the same tub, the cover of the 20 mm ammunition ready-service locker in the inboard side of the tub is visible. Projecting from the outer side of the tub adjacent to the locker is a rack for storing a sixty-round magazine for the 20 mm cannon.

Two men wearing helmets and life vests man the Oerlikon 20 mm cannon on the aft starboard gun tub on SS *John W. Brown*. The gunner is poised with his shoulders snug to the shoulder rests. Above his right hand is the eyepiece of the ring sight. *Richard Thresh*

In a photo taken from the platform between the two aft 3-inch gun tubs, the structure with the slanted side to the lower left is a hatchway leading to the tween deck. The hatch cover for hold number 5 is at the center, flanked on each side by 20 mm gun tubs.

This view off the port stern of SS *John W. Brown* illustrates the arrangement of the ship's aft gun mounts. Over the fantail are two 3-inch/50-caliber guns in circular tubs. Below and aft of them is a single 5-inch/38-caliber gun, also mounted in a tub. *Richard Thresh*

The stern of the *John W. Brown* is displayed, showing the 5-inch/38-caliber gun mount and the port aft 3-inch/50-caliber gun mount. Liberty ships had a single rudder, and the top of the *Brown*'s rudder is protruding from the surface of the water.

The aft deckhouse on the *John W. Brown* served as quarters and also as a foundation for the 5-inch/38-caliber gun mount and tub. This is the starboard side of the aft deckhouse, facing aft. The door provides access to the gunners' quarters. Liberty ships also had a small hospital in this deckhouse. The access ladder leading up to the gun tub has a piece of plywood attached to it, to prevent unauthorized climbing. The 5-inch gun tub lacks the plastic armor found on other gun tubs farther forward on the ship.

The fantail of the SS *John W. Brown* is viewed from the port side, looking aft. In addition to the aft deckhouse, support is provided for the 5-inch gun mount and tub by this locker, as well as several steel posts. The 5-inch gun mount was installed on the *John W. Brown* at the time it was converted to a limited-capacity troopship during World War II. The door on the side of the locker is not watertight and is fitted with a simple padlock hasp and grab handle. Details of the frame underneath the gun tub are visible.

As seen from the front of the platform over the aft deckhouse, a small steam winch by American Hoist & Derrick Company is mounted on the center of the deck. It was used to power a shaft leading to the capstan seen previously, as well as the one in the background.

The steam winch for powering the aft warping capstans is viewed from directly above on the *John W. Brown*. To the left, a driveshaft passes over an open locker and through a bearing; on the end of the shaft is a capstan. To the left is the port bulwark.

Two 3-inch ready-service ammunition lockers are adjacent to a 3-inch/50-caliber gun above the fantail. Dogs with ring-type nuts hold the door of the nearer locker locked shut. On top of the lockers in display cases are two 3-inch rounds.

The fuse setter and pointer's platform is viewed close-up. A crewman made manual settings on the fuse setter. One of the hand cranks was for adjusting the fuse-scale setting, and the other was for engaging and positioning the fuse ring on the nose of the projectile.

The SS *John W. Brown*'s port aft 3-inch/50-caliber gun is displayed. The pointer, in charge of elevating and depressing the gun, sat on this side of the mount. Fastened to the tilted bracket on the rear of the gun platform is the fuse setter.

The pointer's dual handwheels are viewed from the left front of the mount. Above the wheels is the pointer's telescope bracket and telescope. Below the 3-inch/50-caliber gun barrel is the recoil cylinder, and below that is the elevating arc.

The front of the carriage of an aft 3-inch/50-caliber gun on the *John W. Brown* is viewed from the left side of the piece, showing the elevation equipment and the pointer's outboard handwheel. Below the carriage is the gun stand, which is fastened to the deck.

An aft 3-inch/50-caliber gun aboard SS *John W. Brown* is viewed head on. Below the barrel, the large hex nut secures the front of the recoil cylinder to the bracket. Above the pointer's and the trainer's telescopes are their ring sights, used mainly for aerial targets.

The port aft 3-inch/50-caliber gun is viewed from its right-front quarter. On the top of the right side of the carriage, the trunnion is visible. The trunnions were cylindrical projections on each side of the slide and formed the axis for elevation of the gun.

Liberty ships carried 3-inch/50-caliber guns for defense against enemy aircraft or surface craft. This example is currently mounted on SS *Jeeremiah O'Brien*. On the right side of the gun mount are the seat, training (that is, traversing) hand wheel, and ring-and-bead sight for the gun's trainer.

In a close-up of the right side of a 3-inch/50-caliber gun on the *John W. Brown*, the breech housing, breech-operating lever, operating-spring case, recoil cylinder and rod, and elevating arc are in view. To the lower right is the trainer's indicator.

The breech end of the 3-inch/50-caliber gun is displayed. The device at the top center of the photo is the azimuth drum; it is mounted on the L-shaped yoke that also holds the sights and their operating gear. At the bottom left is the fuse setter.

A view of one of the aft 3-inch/50-caliber guns on SS *John W. Brown*, from the left rear, shows the azimuth drum from another angle. The device with the hand crank below the azimuth drum is the elevation drum; the crank is the sight setter's elevation hand control. The sight setter was in charge of adjusting the gun's sights on a target. The curved part with gear teeth on the rear between the bottom of the elevation drum and the elevating arc is the elevation rack. The scooped-out design of the rear of the gun carriage is visible below the gun. To the lower left is the pointer's elevation indicator, above which is his ring sight.
Richard Thresh

The aft part of the SS *Jeremiah O'Brien* is viewed from next to the 5-inch gun on the platform over the fantail. In the foreground are two 20 mm gun tubs. A good view is provided of the rigging of the 5-ton booms arrayed around the mizzenmast.

On a platform above the fantail of SS *John W. Brown* is a single-mount 5-inch/38-caliber gun. This gun has a vertical sliding-wedge breechblock and is manually loaded, but with a powered rammer. The bore of the barrel is 5 inches, and the length of the barrel is 190 inches. The maximum horizontal range, firing a 55-pound projectile, was 18,000 yards, and, when used as an antiaircraft gun, the ceiling was 37,200 feet at 85 degrees of elevation. The rate of fire was between twelve and fifteen rounds per minute. Muzzle velocity averaged around 2,500 feet per second. *Richard Thresh*

The *John W. Brown*'s 5-inch/38-caliber gun mount is viewed from the port side. The fuse setter to the left was capable of setting the fuses of three projectiles; above and beyond it is the pointer's station. He controlled the elevation of the gun. *Richard Thresh*

The 5-inch/38-caliber gun mount on the *Jeremiah O'Brien* lacks the fuse setter. The large casting with the slanted top is called the slide. It is the structure in which the gun's housing (the part aft of the barrel, including the breech) rests, recoils, and elevates.

The fuse setter on the left side of the 5-inch/38-caliber gun mount above the fantail of the SS *John W. Brown* is observed. This device mechanically adjusted the fuses of the 5-inch projectiles to detonate the charge in the projectile at a given time after firing.

The pointer's controls (*left*) and the fuse setter (*right*) on the SS *John W. Brown*'s 5-inch/38-caliber gun are viewed from the front left corner of the mount. In the upper background are the port aft 3-inch gun and its gun tub.

Like the 5-inch/38-caliber gun mount on the *John W. Brown*, this gun mount on the *Jeremiah O'Brien* has a shield across the lower front of the mount. This was to protect the machinery on the front of the mount, including the elevating motor.

The shield on the front of the 5-inch/38-caliber gun mount on the SS *John W. Brown* is shown close-up. The dark, disk-shaped object below the shield is the stand: the circular casting bolted to the deck, upon which the gun carriage and gun are placed.

The *John W. Brown*'s 5-inch/38-caliber gun is viewed from the front, with the top of the shield at the bottom. The pointer's ring sight and controls are on the right in this photo, while the sight and controls of the trainer, who traversed the gun, are to the left.

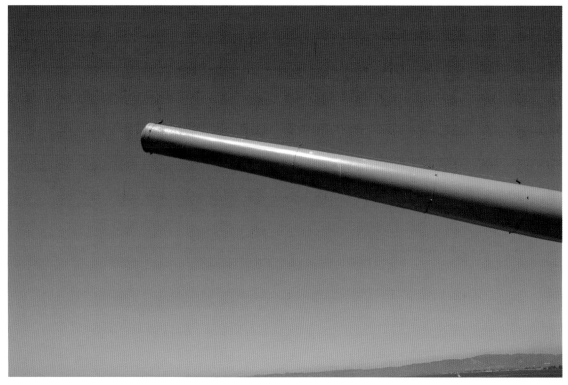

The barrel of the SS *Jeremiah O'Brien*'s 5-inch/38-caliber gun is viewed from the left. Normally, when the gun was not in use, a tompion, or plug, was inserted in the muzzle of the gun. At the command of "Stations," the tompion was removed if it was in place.

The SS *John W. Brown*'s 5-inch/38-caliber gun is observed from the front right quarter, showing the turned-back design of the side of the shield. At the center is the trainer's station. The sight setter stood on the platform with the guardrail when at his station.

In this view of the *John W. Brown*'s 5-inch gun mount from aft, visible on top of the right rear of the slide is the rammer mechanism. The rammerman operated the rammer and stood to the right of it. The gun captain's position was on the deck aft of the gun.

The slide, rammer, breech, and barrel of the 5-inch gun of the *Jeremiah O'Brien* are viewed. To the left is the left side of the gun carriage, at the top of which is the trunnion. Projectiles and powder cartridges were placed in the tray in the foreground for loading.

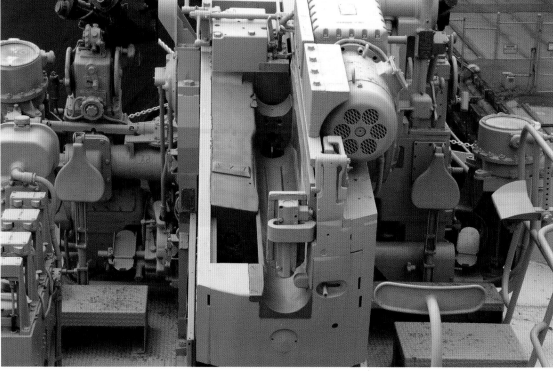

The rear of the 5-inch/38-caliber gun on the *John W. Brown* is viewed. At the center of the photo, suspended above the brass-colored tray, is the hydraulically powered rammer crosshead, which pushed the projectile and powder cartridge into the breech.

A view taken from the rear of the 5-inch/38-caliber gun on the *John W. Brown* shows the brass-colored loading tray and the rammer crosshead (*center foreground*). Also exhibited are the rear of the slide and, to the upper right, the right side of the rammer assembly. *Richard Thresh*

As seen from the rear of the 5-inch/38-caliber gun on the *John W. Brown*, the cylindrical object to the upper right with the holes in the rear is the hydraulic motor for the rammer. In the left background are the pointer's controls and ring sight. Richard Thresh

The fantail of the SS *Jeremiah O'Brien* is viewed from farther forward on the ship. The arrangement of defensive weapons on the fantail was different on this ship than on the *John W. Brown* in that the former had two 20 mm cannons in tubs instead of two 3-inch guns.

The triangular shape of the aft port life-raft rack of the *Jeremiah O'Brien* frames this view of the aft port 20 mm gun tub, with the uncovered 20 mm Oerlikon cannon being visible. Aft of the tub and on the same level is the 5-inch/38-caliber gun mount.

The two aft 20 mm gun tubs of the SS *Jeremiah O'Brien* are observed from the main deck. Between the two gun tubs is an auxiliary steering station, from which the ship could be controlled should the steering system in the wheelhouse fail.

The starboard aft 20 mm gun tub of the *O'Brien* has plastic armor around it. Aft of the cowl ventilator is a warping capstan driven by a driveshaft from a small steam winch at the center of the deck. Forward of the ventilator is a pedestal-mounted fairlead.

A closer view is provided of the aft 20 mm gun tub on the SS *Jeremiah O'Brien*. Mounted on the rails and the front of the platform adjacent to the tub are two diagonally positioned 20 mm gun barrel cooling tubes. Below these tubes are hanging hoses and lines.

In a view across the main deck from the starboard side, forward of the aft deckhouse and gun tubs, parts of the steam winch that powers the warping capstans are visible behind the cowl vent in the foreground. The starboard warping capstan is in the foreground.

Similar to the two 20 mm gun tubs at the front top of the amidships house on the SS *Jeremiah O'Brien*, the aft 20 mm gun tubs are circular in plan and lack the rectangular extensions for accommodating ready-service ammunition lockers.

In a view facing forward from the port side of the gun platform above the fantail of SS *Jeremiah O'Brien*, the rear of the 5-inch/38-caliber gun mount is to the far right, the aft port 20 mm gun and tub are to the left, and the San Francisco skyline is in the distance.

The aft gun platform of the *Jeremiah O'Brien*, formed of nonskid diamond-tread plate, is seen from aft of the starboard 20 mm gun tub. The rear of the loaders' platform of the 5-inch gun is to the left. Between the two 20 mm gun tubs is the auxiliary steering station.

The auxiliary steering station at the front of the aft gun platform of the *Jeremiah O'Brien* includes a wheel, rudder indicator, and, under covers, a binnacle and an engine-order telegraph. The green cover over hold number 5 is in the background

Viewing across the auxiliary steering station from the starboard forward part of the platform over the fantail, in the background is the port aft 20 mm gun. To the left of it is a small davit, presumably for lifting ammunition and other supplies to this level.

The deckhouse on the fantail on the SS *Jeremiah O'Brien* is observed from its forward port quarter. The front of the deckhouse has an application of plastic armor. To the lower left is the aft port warping capstan. Two barrel-cooling tubes are on the upper rails.

A lateral corridor separates the forward and aft parts of the aft deckhouse, situated on the fantail. Stored in the corridor of the SS *Jeremiah O'Brien* are oxyacetylene welding bottles. Also visible in the corridor are a fire plug and hose and a cowl ventilator.

This door on the port side of the aft deckhouse of the *Jeremiah O'Brien* leads into the aft section of the deckhouse, which housed the hospital and gunners' quarters. To the left is a vertical ladder providing access to the gun platform on top of the deckhouse.

On the main deck at the stern aboard SS *Jeremiah O'Brien* are several cable reels and cowl ventilators with screens over the openings. In the background is the rear of the aft deckhouse. Above is the framing underneath the gun platform.

The national colors snap smartly from the flagstaff at the stern of the USS *Jeremiah O'Brien*. The flag is flown from the flagstaff from 0800 hours until sunset while the ship is at anchor. The flagstaff is set at an angle, with the bottom being secured with a pin to a bracket on the deck, and another bracket securing the flagstaff to the upper rail. Also fastened to the upper rail is an anchor light, which was illuminated when the ship was at anchor. This flag bears fifty stars; during World War II, the flags flown by Liberty ships had forty-eight stars.

The aft deckhouse is observed from its forward starboard quarter, showing the position of the starboard aft 20 mm gun tub on the platform above. On the side of the deckhouse is a vertical ladder up to the gun platform, a door, and a porthole.

The cylinder head of the 2,500-horsepower, triple-expansion steam engine of the SS *Jeremiah O'Brien* is observed from above. This contains three cylinders: a high pressure, an intermediate pressure, and a low pressure. To the left is the low-pressure cylinder.

The cylinder head of the *Jeremiah O-Brien*'s engine is viewed from another angle, with the high-pressure cylinder to the right and the medium-pressure cylinder is to the lower left. The red objects are relief valves. To the far right of the assembly is the steam chest.

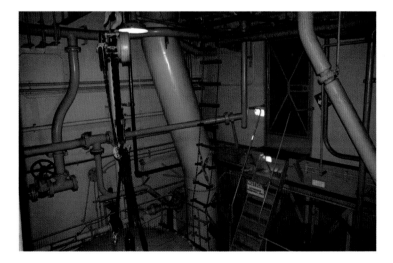

The upper part of the engine room is viewed from a platform toward a door, ladder, and platform on the opposite side of the compartment. On the bulkheads and extending through the space are various water, steam, and electrical lines and pipes.

This view, taken from approximately the same vantage point as the preceding photo, is looking down into the engine room, with the cylinder head visible at the bottom of the photo. The engine was based on a design by the North Eastern Machine Company.

Below the reciprocating engine's cylinders, the bottom of which are at the top of the photo, are the piston rods, connecting rods, and eccentric rods that propel the crankshaft. The three light-colored vertical structures are the columns, which support the cylinders.

At the center is an eccentric rod; there are three sets of eccentric rods on the engine. They are driven by the eccentrics, off-center wheels on the crankshaft, and the eccentric rods cause the engine valves to open and close, thus admitting steam into the cylinders. *Richard Thresh*

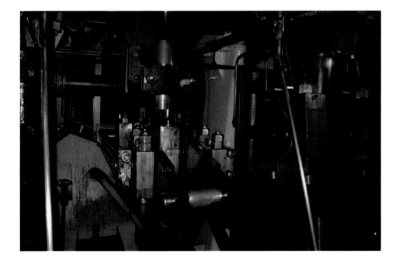

The eccentric rod (*left*) is viewed from another angle, with a piston rod to the upper right. The piston rods are attached to connecting rods via crosshead bearings (the block-shaped assembly to the right), and the connecting rods drive the crankshaft.

Part of the crankshaft of the engine of the SS *Jeremiah O'Brien* is viewed from above. At the center are two eccentrics and eccentric rods. These were mounted in pairs, with one set operating while the engine is moving ahead and one used when in moving astern.

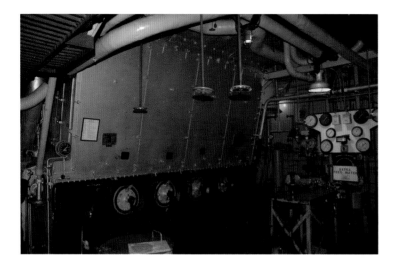

Liberty ships had two boilers with superheaters, based on a Babcock & Wilcox design of the 1890s but modified for oil firing. Despite the age of the design, it was dependable and expedient. This is one of the *Jeremiah O'Brien*'s boilers, with a control panel to the right.

Belowdecks on Liberty ships was an auxiliary steering station; this one is on the SS *Jeremiah O'Brien*. Above the steering wheel is an instrument panel. The ship's steering gear was of a two-cylinder design, powered by a steam engine controlled by a telemotor in the wheelhouse.

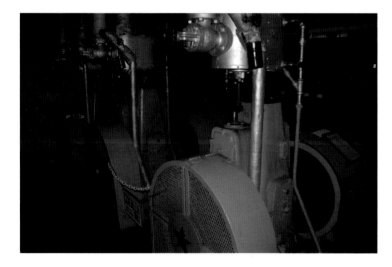

Three 110-volt, 20-kilowatt, 167-amp, direct-current generators, each driven by a single-cylinder reciprocating steam engine, provided electricity for Liberty ships. These are the generators on the *Jeremiah O'Brien*, with the switchboard visible in the background.

This is the main control panel for the USS *John W. Brown*'s generator system. It includes switches and fuses for different compartments and zones of the ship, along with electrical gauges. *Richard Thresh*

One of the SS *John W. Brown*'s cargo holds is viewed from above. As originally built, Liberty ships had five cargo holds, varying in capacity, since hold number 1 had deep tanks below it and thus less height. Hold number 2 had the largest capacity.

When the SS *John W. Brown* was converted to a limited-capacity troopship during World War II, berths for the troops were installed in cargo holds. These bunks are stacked five high and comprise thin mattresses on top of simple frames with bottoms lashed to them.

Quarters on the Liberty ships, such as this one on the SS *Jeremiah O'Brien*, were rudimentary, but not as spartan as those on similarly designed British cargo ships. This one has a hot-water radiator heater, bunk beds, an electric fan, and a locker. *Chris Hughes*

Located at the aft starboard corner of the bridge deck, the captain's stateroom on the SS *Jeremiah O'Brien* has a wooden-framed berth with drawers underneath, closet, seat, bookshelf, clock, wall lamp, and several portholes with curtains. *Chris Hughes*

The officers' mess on a Liberty ship, where these men received their meals, was on the main, or upper, deck at the forward end of the amidships house. This is the officers' mess on the SS *Jeremiah O'Brien*. The refrigerator to the right is a modern addition. *Chris Hughes*

Noticeably more cramped than the officers' mess, the crew's and petty officers' mess on SS *Jeremiah O'Brien* is located on the main deck on the port side of the amidships house. The table has the traditional raised edges to keep plates from sliding off in rough seas.

The galley on a Liberty ship, where meals were prepared, was on the main deck between the engine casing and the boiler casing. The galley range and oven were fueled by oil, and, as an economy measure, stainless-steel fixtures were not used in Liberty ship galleys. *Chris Hughes*

The radio room on the bridge deck of SS *John W. Brown* was the Liberty ship's communications link to the outside world. *From left to right*: a radiotelegraph autoalarm and radiotelegraph transmitters models ET-8024-A and ET-8025. *Richard Thresh*

The wheelhouse of SS *Jeremiah O'Brien* is seen from the starboard side. Both the wheel (*center*) and the engine-order telegraph have shafts leading up to the corresponding controls at the auxiliary steering station, or "monkey island," on the deck above. *Chris Hughes*

The main steering wheel of the *Jeremiah O'Brien* is made of wood and is connected to a telemotor, a device that controls the steering gear belowdecks. To the front of the wheel is the magnetic compass binnacle. It is traditional to paint wheelhouse floors red.

Though they were unglamorous and somewhat ungainly in appearance, the Liberty ships provided an indispensable service, transporting supplies and materials essential for the continuation of the war from the United States to distant shores. SS *Jeremiah O'Brien* is a testament to that breed of cargo ships that helped win World War II.